Crazy Blues

The Gift of Empowerment

Rhonda J. Lewis

ACKNOWLEDGEMENTS

I give honor and praise to the Most High God Our Lord and Savior Jesus Christ. Thank you Father for never forsaking me in my season of Blues.   In my time of long suffering, pain, heartbreak, child molestation as young girl, abortions as a teenager, substance abuse, family domestic abuse, adultery, spiritual abuse, divorces, and domestic violence, Father you gave me the Holy Spirit to comfort me, you gave me strength, your presence saved my life. Abba Father Thank you for depositing your gifts, and your guidance, your protection and eternal love in my heart. Thank you for your overwhelming Joy and YOUR GLORY!!

Acknowledgments

To my special friend Terry "Harmonica" Bean, who continues to teach the young millenniums about the history of Blues, he taught me so much about the history of Mississippi Blues, spiritual songs and the connection between gospel blues and blues. His love of God's people is a gift to the world. He says "the blues brings people together" and in these day and times that's very important. He says "Do what makes you happy, keep dancing Dancing Lady, I Love you Ba Bee"!

Acknowledgments

I want to acknowledge Pastor John P. Kee for always declaring and decreeing health and prosperity over his Partakers and showing his continued love for his community.

Pastor Kathleen Heck at Flowing River Church in Clearwater Florida, your prophetic word over my flag dance ministry, your prophetic teaching on healing and deliverance, your food pantry, and especially showing God's love for all people!

To my mother Deborah Wilson, in Dayton Ohio, who always says "I love you more", and continues to be a special part of my life and my Hero! I love you Mom!

Acknowledgments

To my Grandma Rose who was challenged with hearing at 94 years young, a prayer warrior, she always prayed for health and strength, long suffering never stops her. She listened when I called in the midnight hours, her voice was like chocolate when   she talked about her blues. She told me to keep praying Pray Until Something Happens.

Acknowledgments

Elias Antonas Prophetic Missionary in Clearwater Florida thank you for your teaching on the prophetic.

Dedication

This book is dedicated to the God of Healing and The God who Delivers us from pain and suffering, bringing joy in the morning. The God who battles for you and me, the Almighty God.

Thank you, Lord, for seeing my worth as a precious jewel. Thank you for your gift. You chose me before I was born, you new my name before I was born, and anointed me to flag dance, minister unto the Lord in flag dance and break yokes!

Dedication

To my courageous sons William K. Vauls II, Jake D. Nealy, and Perry L. Nealy, who always believed in me. My handsome grandsons and beautiful granddaughters Kamal R. Vauls, Kaseem R. Vauls, Kenneth R. Vauls, Keiron R. Vauls, Keishon River Vauls, Kruz R. Vauls, Randall Jake Nealy and Alexander Nealy V., my granddaughters, Kimora Rose Vauls, Kelani Vauls, Chloe Nealy, Serenity Nealy and Jordan Williams. Always reach for the stars, this book is for you!

INTRODUCTION

The Purpose of this book, is to help you the reader see God's heart and movements in what appears to be craziness. God has instructed the Holy Spirit to guide us through it all, if we can only sit still long enough to listen for his peace. You the reader will gain knowledge of how the use of spirituals, blues music, movements, groans, and hollers in the dance is becomes deliverance and heals the human spirit and soul. It is how historically the Blues was played outside of the churches but went into the church to strengthen the soul and spirit of black people who are a broken people. The book of Lamentations, the Book of Psalms, David, and the Seer Prophets spoke of the blues and how seeing God's glory in the blues provided revelation of healing.

Preface

God always interrupted me when I got lost in my own crazy blues. It was normal for me see drama all around me until one day I heard the LORD say "I WILL LOVE YOU MORE THAN ANY MAN", and his voice was like thunder in small apartment bathroom.   I had been crying tears of the blues, but I need to say this was only after surviving years of emotional abuse, generational domestic violence, substance abuse, two marriages which ended in divorce, including a child custody battle, being charged with and locked up for kidnapping my own sons from my second husband, fighting Ohio's backward legal system and privileged people with dirty money, the blues was apart of my life.

I grew up in a small southwestern city country town called Dayton, Ohio just 30 minutes north of Cincinnati, Ohio. Dayton is known for Funk music. I grew up in the 70's and 80's and 90's around great musician like Ohio Players' Leroy Sugarfoot Bonner singing "Fire," I Wanna be Free," Funky Worm,", Mark Hicks of Slave, Roger Troutman & The Zapp Band with songs like "More Bounce to the Ounce," Heartbreaker," "Computer Love" and my special friend Larry Troutman was my good friend of ten years, I saw his love of investing in the Gem City, and his love of playing the African congas inspired him and me in my time of blues.

In my younger years the 60's and 70's, I heard Rhythm & Blues artists like The Isley Brothers, "It's Your Thang," Jackie Wilson "Your Love Keeps lifting Me", James Brown's "A Mans World", Sam Cooke's "A Change is Gone Come". Those were the good old days, inspired by Gospel and the Blues, growing up in some crazy blues times.

It was Rhythm & Blues Monday through Saturday night in my house, and on most Sunday's I was at Grandma's house, I remember it was gospel artists like The Clark Sister's singing Endow Me or CeeCee Winan's music gave me a special feeling I danced, it made me cry. At Grandma's she loved listening to BB King's, "The Thrill Is Gone", KoKo Taylor's "I'm a Woman", Howlin Wolf's "Chocolate Drop". Grandma used to dance her signature dance called the "Hully Gully" to it, whenever it came on the radio and sang it to me. I later discovered who KoKo Taylor and Howlin Wolf were, I can still hear her call me her "Chocolate Drop". Grandma is gone home to see the Lord now. Thank you God for Sunday's at Grandma's house, peace and deliverance from a broken heart. I believe God who is the Author and Finisher of my life has place this book on my heart to share.   I pray that is will will inspire many to see through the crazy blues and look for God's glory in the craziness of it all.

Okay so, What is the Blues?

"You got the blues when your man is cheatin in town on you!"
KoKo Taylor, Blues Singer

"When my girl wants Champagne & Reefer"
Muddy Waters, Harmonist, Blues Musician

"When you can tell your good man don't want to be around you no mo."
Ida Goodman, Pianist, Blues & Gospel Singer

"When you aint heard from your girl in three days"
Floyd Lee Band

"Hard times, aint got no shoes on my feet. "
John Lee Hooker

The Crazy Blues
The Crazy Blues is a state of mind, a bad relationship experience you cant escape, a pain, a sorrow, a joy lost and we all have had the blues and will continue to have some kind of blues. It is a black music genre and musical form which was originated around 1860's by Blacks brought over from Africa, from roots in Africa " a musical tradition".

The Legendary Mamie Smith sings about the Crazy Blues

"Crazy Blues" is a song, renamed from another song named "Harlem Blues". Mamie Smith and her band recorded it on August 10th, 1920, which was released by Okeh Records. Perry Bradford a composer and pianist claimed to have played piano on the recording, back then it sold 75,00 copies. There were many recordings with the blues in the titles this recording was the first significant hit recording by a black artist. The record of blues made Mamie Smith the first female artist of a blues record. The success of "Crazy blues" opened up the race record market, for the first time major record companies started producing records with and black buyer in mind. "Crazy blues" was entered into the Grammy Hall of Fame in 1994.

God's Glory Work

I believe God used Mamie Smith to be the first black female blues recording artist. When she shouted "Crazy Blues" and Perry Bradford was a pianist and composer of blues, he heard her and talked with the white recording companies, he got them to make a record it in the 1920's, my God, the music was sold in black neighborhoods only, until Elvis Presley made a name for himself by copying the sounds of legendary blues singers.

Even through blues music the voice of God can speak what to share. Yes giving God the glory, there can be healing in singing the blues. Even then blacks were going through it. Singing in the church on Sunday and all through the week finding work in the shows on steamboats going up and down the rivers just singing the blues.

God used women like Bessie Robinson a.k.a Bessie Smith, Mae Barns a Dancer, Mamie Smith, Ida Goodman and Singer, KoKo Taylor, Blues Queen, and Ma Rainey to travel the country and world with their style to different regions to share their secrets. Ma Rainey captured the pubic eyes.

What Legendary Women of the Blues have said about the Blues

The legendary Ida Goodman said " I could be playing the blues, I can feel something all over me, and the next I know I be feeling good.   Then I can play the church version same song and can feel like the devil is in me. But then you play it again the church song and that christian feeling come back to you.   That's just the way it is. God has his glory work and the devil got his.

The Meaning of God's Glory

While I'm shouting "glorrray" right now, at church it can indeed indicate praise, but a close study of its use in the Old Testament reveals an altogether different meaning, one that conveys the original understanding of its form and function.

"Glory" is one of the most common praise words in scripture. In the Hebrew Bible, gloryis expressed with several Hebrew words; including Hod and kavod.   Later the original Hebrew Bible for glory were translated iin Christian Bible as the Greek word doxa.

The Hebrew word kavod (K-V-D) has means IMPORTANT, WEIGHT, DEFERENCE OR HEAVINESS" but primarily kavod means "GLORY, RESPECT", "HONOR" and "MAJESTY".

The word glory is used 148 times in Genesis, Exodus, Leviticus and Numbers, and from Deuteronomy to Malachi. In the Old Testament, glory has two entirely unrelated meanings and describes two completely different ideas.

I believe God "sees me and you in our Blues and feels our **blues" and as David expressed** in the bible, the book of Lamentation, the book of Psalms in different verses God can feel injustices or your expressions for better life and lost loves, jobs, and money This I know!

Father God, You already know my Blues
I Pray Father God you are God of Healing, the
Jehovah El Roi, and The God Who Sees All
that my testimony be like a catapult to someone, be
a blessing and an inspirational tool for any woman
or man who is victim to domestic violence,
physical abuse and struggling to find your way out
of the relationship. I pray that you see the will of
God and His glory in your blues. I know and am
certain that God will make a way of escape! I pray
for the children who are witnessing family
domestic violence, I pray that children be protected
in the midst of this evilness. I surrendered my heart
and soul to God, received Salvation of Jesus Christ
and baptized in the name of Jesus Christ, and the
fire of the Holy Spirit, I pray that you walk with
my Father God, I know He walks with you and
your family. I thank you Father, that today I know
You are walking with me. Amen!

Give God the glory!

It is written:

Nations will see your righteousness, and all kings your glory. You will be called by a new name that the mouth of the LORD will bestow. You will be a crown of glory in the hand of the LORD, a royal diadem in the palm of your God.

To grant to those who mourn in Zion— to give them a beautiful headdress instead of ashes, the oil of gladness instead of mourning, the garment of praise instead of a faint spirit; that they may be called oaks of righteousness, the planting of the LORD, that he may be glorified.

Isaiah 61:3

FUNK and BLUES IN the GEM CITY

Growing up in the North Midwestern part of the United States in Dayton, Ohio back in the 70's, 80's and 90's, bands like Lakeside, Slave, Ohio Players,Atlantic Starr, The Dazz Band, Midnight Star, Shalamar, The Deele, and the Zapp Band, I spent my weekends biking or walking along the bank's edge of Wolf Creek to the Little Miami River and over to Grandma's house listening to music in my head to escape and I mean escape my family, the family domestic violence and daily arguing.   Grandma's house was my house of refuge, once there feeling safe and at peace. I remember looking up to the sky while riding my bike and praying to God saying "Please God keep my mommy safe". I didn't know how to pray then, but I knew God heard me, I felt like God watched over me, God was right there with me, as if the sky was surrounding me, the white clouds were following me.

Women Got the Blues

In the late 1960's women had no rights.   I mean, men believed to gain power over women and control over their spouse, wife or woman they literally beat the woman's ass. Domestic violence in some families was a learned behavior, it is not caused by anger, mental problems, drugs or alcohol. This was done to break a male black slave owned by a white slave owner.   This trait was passed down in his family to three and four generations.

How Children Get the Blues

Children and youth who are exposed to domestic violence experience emotional, mental and social damage that can affect their developmental growth and some children lose the ability to feel empathy for others.

From the late 1960's and 1970's it seemed everywhere I looked people had the blues. During these times while 82% percent of heroin users in the 1960's were men. As time went on things started to feel crazy normal. The normal was Dad addicted to heroin he had the mean blues. I saw his highs and lows from using heroin.

As a 5 years old when my young eyes witnessed a physical fight between my parents. I witnessed my mother being strangled, seeing her keep my father from trying to stab her with a butcher knife, he pinned her down, and she fought for her life. I was traumatized, I had the blues already imprinted in my head.   Born into the blues, I was 13 years old, when I witnessed my mother being whipped with a belt by my father, he had just moved back in, I remember feeling helpless again, only being able to scream, I had already developed Post Traumatic Stress Disorder along with anxiety whenever hostile situations in social gatherings happened. My mind played the blues song "Daddy please don't hurt her, please stop, don't hit her again!

Families Got the Crazy Blues

In the late 70's one evening my father left me at home with his friend of the family, I guess he never thought a male friend of the family would think of touching his 13 year old stepdaughter, while he went to pick up my mom from work.   The pervert did the unexpected. Yes, I was mishandled, touched inappropriately, newly formed breast fondled. I was mishandled and traumatized. He was my father's cousin. Later that year the child molester was found dead from a heroin drug overdose. The bible speaks of the spirit of perverseness being an iniquity a sin, but that is a whole another book.

For we do not wrestle against flesh and blood, but against the rulers, against the authorities, against the cosmic powers over this present darkness, against the spiritual forces of evil in the heavenly places.Ephesians 6:12

I started using drugs at 14, smoking reefer before class with an uncle, using with friends at school and eventually started failing classes in my freshman year of high school. The following year I thought I had found the love of my life, someone to rescue me. He was handsome, a high school football player, and a very good dancer! I became sexually active at 15 and pregnant at 15 years old, afraid to tell my father, afraid of what might happen, so afraid that I had an abortion…I didn't understand then, I had opened doors of rejection, loneliness, emotional pain, immoralization and the spirit of perverseness attacking me!

A Lack of Understanding

Now, suffering from undiagnosed Post Traumatic Stress Disorder and Anxiety terrified to hear what my father might say once he found this out. I shut myself in my room every evening and cried myself to sleep in silence, I was filled with grief, guilt and shame, I had no one to talk to about this I became depressed and rebellious. I didn't want to live anymore, but God saved my life.

Our lack of understanding of soul ties and how unwanted touches as children can open the door to iniquity and destroy your own soul. The energy of a sexual acts or lack of understanding about an orgasm can affect the body and soul and open spiritual portals to have human beings tied and bonded to one another other.

Not only did this happen to me, but it happened to so many other families, young women, and young men, our ancestors were raped, our aunts had vicious acts of sexual torment which happened in the cotton fields and cornfields. Babies born out of wedlock from perverted acts within the family, or from intimate violence such as date rapes, all of this steaming from the mishandling by slave masters and generational iniquities, and spiritual soul ties. Today some babies, I said some, are born out of generational transgressions, iniquities from family secrets which were kept. The blues crept in from the air.

Father I thank you, Upon you I have leaned from before my birth; You are he who took me from my mother's womb. My praise is continually of you.   Psalm 71:6

Little Miami River Blues

At 16, I became pregnant, I would walk 4 miles from my home, down the Little Miami River's edge looking into the the sky with my eyes on the LORD, singing to him along the way to Paul Laurence Dunbar House on Edison Street, walking towards Broadway Street to find some sense of peace after a four mile walk along the river's edge to the home of my teenage boyfriend. As I walked the river's edge on the trail, silence penetrated the air, the smell of lavender penetrated my nostrils, and a warmth in my heart was overwhelming. I could feel the glory presence of God's glory was with me as I talked to God and sang my blues, the feeling of worthlessness had melted into the waters.

It is written: *The voice of the LORD is upon the waters; The God of glory thunders, The LORD is over many waters.   Psalm 29:3*

The church blues and the Blues

Back in the 1950's a lot of women left the church because they too were being sexually abused by pastors and their Christian husbands.Church folks called it devils music, most women blues musicians or singers were Baptist and came right out the Baptist church. Having parents who were preachers, the Christian woman were of society groups and would sing it when people could not talk about their life of abuse or love gone wrong.

The Author's Belief

And it came to pass when the evil spirit from God was upon Saul, that David took a harp, and played with his hand; So Saul was refreshed, and was well, and the evil spirit departed from him."
1 Samuel 16:23

And David danced before the Lord with all his might, wearing priestly garments.   So David and all the people of Israel brought up the Ark of the Lord with shouts of joy and the blowing of rams horns.
2 Samuel 6:14-15

But now, bring the harpist" and while he the harpist played, the hand of the Lord came upon Elisha.
2 King 3:5

I was dancing before the LORD who chose me above your father and his family.   He appointed me as the leader of Israel the people of the LORD, so I celebrate

before the LORD yes and I am willing to look even more foolish than this.
2 Samuel 6:22

God's musical militia

This sound was born in the deep south over one hundred years ago..that swept across the land. This was the folk music of those who had been abused and mistreated and it carried the cries for freedom, justice and equality of a oppressed people.

This sound was the sowed pain and trauma, "the Lord is bringing redemption and healing. The despair and hopelessness that gave birth to the blues are being replaced.

- Traditionally, glory is understood to mean "praise for the Lord."

Glory in the blues is what happens when you hear and see the call, obey, serve up your gifts and talents, and walk out your heavenly assignments with others.

BREAKTHROUGH IN THE BLUES

God's glory breaks forth among his people and brings the Ark home. For many people, the effects of a past traumatic event don't go away until there is a breakthrough. Jesus lamented and cried the blues, David danced before the Lord with all his might, he was a man after Gods' own heart and God chose him over other appointed men. So we too should dance and turn our mourning into dancing.

Glory in times of Craziness

Now to him who is able to do immeasurably more than all we ask or imagine, according to his power that is at work within us, to him be glory in the church and in Christ Jesus throughout all generations, for ever and ever! Amen Ephesian 3:20.

No longer will you be called Forsaken, nor your land named Desolate; but you will be called Hephzibah, and your land Beulah; for the LORD will take delight in you, and your land will be His bride....Isaiah 62:3

May The Lord bless you and keep you; the Lord make his face shine on you and be gracious to you; the Lord turn his face toward you and give you peace.

Numbers 6:24-26

Be Sober minded and be watchful

The spirit of familiarity, for a brief time there was chaos in peace.. At 16 years old, I became severely depressed every chance I got I started running away to dance club with my baby's daddy. He was very jealous, verbally abusive and physically abusive, this was familiar to me and as crazy as this sounds, I loved him.

It is written:
Be sober-minded; be watchful. Your adversary the devil prowls around like a roaring lion, seeking someone to devour.

A Sober Mind

I remember on the weekends pregnant and dancing at Grandma's house with my aunt and uncles, my mother's brothers and sister, making up dance routines to music of that time. In my mind I was the musician, singer, and dancer. The songs of love and blues was my life. I became pregnant again and making my way over to Broadway Street, walking past Paul Laurence Dunbar's house near Williams Street, the city has renamed this area now it's now called Wolf Creek, back in the days it was called the West Side, before the city of Dayton.

Negative Impact Gentrification

Changing Times and Gentrification, at 16 years old I didn't realize what was happening, I only heard about "Miss Nellie" my grandma's neighbor was selling there property, selling there homes, they were forced to sell!

As the demand for an area increasing, and the higher income earners come into the area, gentrification can be off set by allowing redevelopment that the new more affluent population, by pushing out the black people.

They keep taken our property and land!

My question was "How can we keep our property"? The city planners wanted my safe haven, they told the homeowners a lie "their properties were no longer valuable" or either their properties were not worth what they had invested in them and they had no rights to keep their land and property. Dayton had planned an "Eminent Domain" and "Gentrification" of the West Side long before the West side even knew about it. I saw how Grandma fought to keep her inheritance from her father,

I saw her courage how she fought for what she thought was a fair price for her inheritance, her father's property.

A good man and woman leaves an inheritance to his children's children, And the wealth of the sinner is stored up for the righteous. Proverbs 13:22

On that day the LORD their God will save them as the flock of His people; for like jewels in a crown, they will sparkle over His land.
Zechariah 9:16

Grandma had the Blues

Gentrification, was Grandma's blues. Her house was her father's house. The city eventually plowed down the entire neighborhood, street no longer looked the same, Fitch Street, Broadway Street, Fifth Street, building after building of black owned establishments which once were my safe haven from a vicious and cruel world were now gone, destroyed. I cried the blues and prayed to God even more.   But God, God fought for her. She later moved to the Northwest side of Dayton Ohio, which then was called the "Golden Triangle.

The Lord gives the command; a great company of women proclaim it:
Psalm 68:11

GOD a HEALER in the Blues song!

Singing for Deliverance

From The Beginning women of African Slavery sang Spiritual Songs, Work Songs meant singing the Blues. Work Songs The song of black slaves represented the tears of slaves who were captured and enslaved and physically abused. The first book ever to be published about Spiritual Slave songs of the United States, publishes in 1867.   There isn't a system to preserve our inheritances. African Americans sang songs from the beginning, this was born from blacks being stripped from there identity and forced to live in a land unknown.

Communication in the cornfields and cotton fields

From long suffering in the cotton fields, slaves began to sing and communicate through the song, making code words to mention subject that were off limits.

Code words to talk about subject that were off limits. Black people were hired to sing at their slave master's private parties where the white masters would watch their slaves be made into male prostitutes, and slave prostitutes for dignitaries in the south, states like Mississippi, Alabama, Louisiana, Georgia, and Texas just to name a few Blacks had to and were expected to sing to their masters.

Prayers for Deliverance

The slander and murmuring of my assailants against me all day long.   When they sit and when they rise, see how they mock me in song.   You will pay them back what they deserve, O LORD, according to the work of their hands. Lamentations 3:63

As it is written in the bible:
And I will give unto thee the keys of the kingdom of heaven: and whatsoever thou shalt bind on earth shall be bound in heaven: and whatsoever thou shalt loose on earth shall be loosed in heaven. Matthew 16:19

Singing songs of lamentation, cornfield hollers, personal struggles and the lamenting unto the LORD.

Deliverance songs is one of the biggest influences for blacks today in the world.   Yes, while slaves tailored the songs into Spirituals, slaves took the long sufferings and made songs, songs of hardships and struggle, songs of repentance.

By Bill Withers A Song to His Glory, Lean On Me

Sometimes in our lives we all have pain
We all have sorrow
But if we are wise
We know that there's always tomorrow

Lean on me, when you're not strong
And I'll be your friend
I'll help you carry on
For it won't be long
'Til I'm gonna need
Somebody to lean on

Please swallow your pride
If I have things you need to borrow
For no one can fill those of your needs
That you won't let show

You just call on me brother, when you need a hand
We all need somebody to lean on
I just might have a problem that you'll understand
We all need somebody to lean on

Lean on me, when you're not strong
And I'll be your friend
I'll help you carry on
For it won't be long
'Til I'm gonna need
Somebody to lean on

You just call on me brother, when you need a hand
We all need somebody to lean on

I just might have a problem that you'll understand
We all need somebody to lean on

If there is a load you have to bear
That you can't carry
I'm right up the road
I'll share your load

If you just call me (call me)
If you need a friend (call me) call me uh huh (call me) if
you need a friend

(call me)

If you ever need a friend (call me)
Call me (call me) call me (call me) call

me
(Call me) call me (call me) if you need a friend

(Call me) call me (call me) call me (call me) call me (call
me) call me (call me)

Upon you LORD I have leaned on from before my birth; you are he who took me from my mother's womb. My praise is continually of you. Psalm 71:6

Deliverance From Heartbreak

I learned how to deal with being home on the weekends, for six months I prayed and talked to God. I had the blues the entire year and I fought with my baby's father daily. I stayed home from school until the birth of my first son, he was the most beautiful baby I had ever seen a handsome gift from God. I survived the blues by dancing unto the Lord. I survived domestic violence. I was delivered from many abusive relationships, many nights of crying the blues, and many many nights of crying out, praying and pleading the blood of Jesus over my sons, family and my life. Today I know God has healed my heart but not without the protection of my Lord and Savior Jesus Christ

Take some time to meditate on The LORD and all He has done.
5 Ways to BEAT THE BLUES:

1.

2.

3.

4.

5.

**Words from Terry Harmonica Bean
Blues Historian, Mississippi Hill Country
Blues Musician says;**

"When they brought Quotes *he slaves into this country
from Africa, they brought the blues over, too. When the
slaves were freed and they went their separate ways, the
blues went with them and spread all over these United
States … it was the black
man's music," he said. "But here in Mississippi,
something different was happening.*

Quotes by Terry Harmonica Bean

*"They play the blues down here and they also play
gospel down here, too. And a lot of the church folks
told me, 'You know, Terry, the blues came from the
church. And I say, 'No, man.' My grandmother died at
105 years old and I used to talk to her about that. She
said, 'Son, the blues came from the fields and then went
to the church.' She always told me that when she was a
little-bitty girl, people were playing the blues in the
fields and the folks in the church did not have no
music.*

The people that were out playing those juke joints all night long had the fear put into them, so they started going to church and they started playing music in the church. They were all blues players and now they're playing the blues in church.

A lot of Christian people don't want to admit that's how it is, but the blues came from the fields and went to the church. But I always tell people, if you're playing music and it ain't got no blues in it, you're really not playing no music."

Terry Harmonica Bean

"If there wasn't no music, there sho nuff would be some troubles goin' on". The Blues is in our history, it's a spiritual thing! "Black slaves were forced to attend white churches were they were forced to learn white Christianity."

Terry Harmonica Bean

African Americans were forced to learn from white slave owners, but they survived by singing the songs of their slavery which became the blues.

Real Talk: Terry "Harmonica" Bean

Blues Historian and Blues Musician talked about how African dance and African sounds are rooted in our DNA. I personally have seen how it truly ministers to thousands who listen to him play his harmonica, those who can receive what their eyes see and their ears hear are moved in that instant. He said many times those that came before him and how his father Mr. Eddie Bean and many others got their names christened on the Blues Hall of Fame forever.

Mr. Bean is a bit old fashioned but his Godly words are true and his righteous spirit almost burst out, talks louder than his harmonica can play, at times. He plays sounds that speak of his past hurts, and simultaneously playing from old tears of joy. He is a righteous man like David after God's very own heart.

In an interview he said, "People always say, 'Man, you think a lot of your grandparents, don't you?' And I do. I live off a lot of the stuff that they told me. People want to call it old-fashioned or something and I say, 'Look, you can call it what you want, but I still use a lot of the mentality that they taught to me,'" he said. "That's what works for me and it always has. We (people today) really don't know how good we've got it and what all our parents had to go through to make sure we do have it good these days.""I've had a great year. When the good Lord let's you do what you're doing and be here on top of the ground, you're having a great year," he said. "I had to go to play the blues for a lot of people.

I was in Spain, Germany, France, Belgium, Scotland, Denmark … I was just tickled to death with the way things went for me this year." Yes, I've been tempted to try some of that stuff, but the reason I won't do it is because keeping the blues alive is my thing … the delta blues and the hill country blues … that's my thing. That's the stuff that carries me all around the world," he said. "All that other stuff is alright, but it ain't the real deal, you know what I'm saying? And let me tell you, the real deal works for me.

A lot of people don't realize this, but all that rap, hip-hop and rock stuff, that's all music that is off the branches of the blues' tree. The real-deal blues are like Johnson grass or maybe Kudzu, it may die out over here, but it'll pop up over yonder. It ain't ever going to die out. That's kinda' the case with me. It looked like there wasn't a lot of young black guys playing the blues and then I popped up." "I try to encourage a lot of young people – black and white – to carry on the tradition of the blues. It seems like a lot of blacks are really not into the blues these days because they don't really understand it. They think it's depressing, but it's not, man. They just need to try to understand it. I talk to a lot of young blacks about the stuff they do, like getting into all kinds of trouble because they want attention. And I understand that. I used to be a young fella' myself. But I chose music to get my attention and you also get paid for it, too. That way, you ain't got to go out and kill nobody to get attention."

PRAISE GOD EVEN IN YOUR BLUES

Praise Him with tambourine and dancing; praise Him with the strings and flute.
Psalm 150:4

And David, wearing a linen ephod, danced with all his might before the LORD.

2 Samuel 6:14

ANOINTED IN YOUR BLUES

African Dance has influenced many **dance** forms, such as hip-hop. Throughout **history, Africans** performed **dances** to celebrate a birth, harvest or death. Communities relied on **dance** to ward off evil spirits, to ask the gods for prosperity, or to resolve conflict.

It brings to life the past right before my eyes and confirms what Mother Marie Jackson and Mother Ida Hogue would say and spoke about, "Honey you are anointed to dance", and they would say "someone can be anointed by God to dance or play music and that sound is so moving or that particular movement with the flags, it touches your pain, heals it and brings joy and healing in that very moment."

Today, I use flags in my dance as a healing tool and I allow the Holy Spirit to choose the song. I listen and understand it is rooted in African beat, the healing sound, the drums, guitar and heritage, the knowledge that body and mind are inseparable on a spiritual and physical level, providing feelings of unity, harmony, and breakthrough.

For many people, the effects of a past traumatic event don't go away. God lamented and cried the blues too.

And the Word became flesh, and dwelt among us, and we saw His glory, glory as of the only begotten from the Father, full of grace and truth.
John 1:14

Fredrick Douglas wrote:
"The songs of slaves represented their sorrows, and tears of joy.

The story of Blues is often narrated as black culture laying the brass-tacks to an eternity of prominence and influence in the American society. Blues talks about betrayal, sadness, misfortune, and regrets. The Blues also talks about getting over the sadness, and looking forward to a brighter tomorrow.

Dancing In God's Glory
You turned my wailing into dancing, you removed my sackcloth and clothed me with joy, that my heart may sing your praises and not be silent. LORD my GOD I will praise you forever.
Psalm 30:11-12

Jesus said to her, "Did I not say to you that if you would believe you would see the glory of God?"

John 11:40

You said, 'Behold, the LORD our God has shown us His glory and His greatness, and we have heard His voice from the midst of the fire; we have seen today that God speaks with man, yet he lives. Deuteronomy 5:24

Encountering God's Glory In The Crazy Blues

One thing have I desired of the LORD, that will I seek after; that I may dwell in the house of the LORD all the days of my life, to behold the beauty of the LORD, and to inquire in his temple. Psalm 27:4

But we all, with unveiled face, beholding as in a mirror the glory of the Lord, are being transformed into the same image from glory to glory, just as from the Lord, the Spirit.

2 Corinthians 3:18

The glory of God is like a spiritual dance and spiritual music that celebrates and moves mountains when you allow God to take over.

Blues is like "pleasure and success" through the mighty power of God under the direction and guidance of the

Holy Spirit. Today, as I listen to those enlisted, who got their names in the Blues Hall of Fame forever, paying tribute to those who transformed Blues into what it is today.

LAMENTATIONS THE BOOK OF BLUES

The Book of Lamentations to the late sixth century B.C., when Babylonia attacked the Kingdom of Judah and thousands of ancient "Hebrew POWs" were forcibly exiled to Babylon, which is today modern Iraq and Syria. He called the exile one of the "greatest watershed" events in all of biblical history. "Arguably one of the most emotionally wrenching books of the Bible is the five chapters we call the Book of Lamentations," he said. "They are cries of anguish from the ruins of defeated Jerusalem after the devastation of Nebuchadnezzar's army who ravished Jerusalem and the surrounding villages of Judah. "But these books were more than just the first horrifying scream after the dreadful attack. They are very unusual calls that were very carefully and artfully composed. If blues come from the suffering and pain of a people, then Lamentations in a powerful sense is: Hebrew Blues!

The Slave Blues

African's likewise suffered horrendously under centuries of domestic violence from America's slavery. Ironically, in some case to their own powerful interpretation of Christianity, the very religion under which they were enslaved, super natural faith was undeniable and spoken about in their coded lyrics.

These songs and stories were about how black people young and old pulled from a higher power and danced.

No evil will befall you, no plague will approach your tent.
Psalm 91:10

So we too should dance and turn our mourning into dancing. Isaiah 61:1-3

David danced before the Lord with all his might, he was a man after Gods' own heart and God chose him over other appointed men

The Divine Blues

We give witness and testimony to how men and women were found giving God the glory after being hospitalized for a virus. The victorious spirit of blues or divine blues can be recognized as God's protection which strengthened us during times of near death. God continues daily to fight for us, and we recover.

Divine Blues

Yes, after my third marriage of 15 years ended in divorce I moved to Charlotte North Carolina attended New Life Fellowship under the teaching of Pastor John P. Kee for 8 years, where God gifted me with the gift of speaking with tongues, witnessing the call on my life, he ordained me as a Minister of Flags to minister to the church and nations. I believe movements are a prophetic artistic worship, an expression of love to GOD and use the dance, gospel blues to dance, and communicate to God, and praying for others simultaneously to instantaneously heal broken hearts. I believe, if David danced with all his heart unto God and move God, In the name of Jesus! So can we! Dance Movement and Flags are used as tools in the gift of healing, because they unify the body of Christ.

Yes, even today in these times, the crazy blues continues to test our faith as we call on Jesus Christ to help build your faith, so that you may see the glory of God. Continue to seek God's face, pray for the miracles and look for signs and wonders to heal us and our nations.

Some of the things you went through, was simply so God could loose you!
Pastor John P. Kee
Glory Hallelujah!

It is written:
God did extraordinary miracles through Paul. I believe, so that even handkerchiefs or aprons that had touched his skin were carried away to the sick, and their diseases left them and the evil spirits came out of them.

When Jesus heard this, He said, "This sickness will not end in death. No, it is for the glory of God, so that the Son of God may be glorified through it."
John 11:40

Even in these times, we keep our distance in times of social distancing, we keep pressing even when it changes our way of communicating.   This new normal is changing our way of living again, the old way of coming together to strengthen our families is of the past. They tell us to keep moving even when everything around us looks unsafe, be wise, observe how the world is changing right before our eyes, "keep your distance" during these times of crisis will certainly test our faith.

If you fully obey the Lord your God and carefully follow all his commands I give you today, the Lord your God will set you high above all the nations on earth. All these blessings will come on You will be blessed in the city and blessed in the country.

The fruit of your womb will be blessed, and the crops of your land and the young of your livestock-the calves of your herds and the lambs of your flocks. Your basket and your kneading trough will be blessed.
Deuteronomy 28:1-5

And as for you, the anointing which you received from Him abides in you, and you have no need for anyone to teach you, but as His anointing teaches you about all things, and is true and is not a lie, and just as it has taught you, you abide in Him"
1 John 2:27

The anointing gives you unusual contacts

It connects you with men of great caliber, men of the Spirit, people of influence and people that God has ordained to be great and mighty.

Now the Lord is the Spirit, and where the Spirit of the Lord is, there is freedom.2 Corinthians 3:17

John 2:11

It is written in the bible: Men and women will dance and be glad, young men and old as well. I will turn their mourning into gladness. For his anger is but for a moment, and his favor is for a lifetime. Weeping may tarry for the night, but joy comes with the morning.

Psalm 30:5

The Author's Belief

He only is my rock and my salvation: he is my defense; You shall not be moved.

WRITE YOUR THOUGHTS AND CONFESSIONS.

AFIRM Your belief in GOD, in these crazy times?

Write your thoughts.

In God is my salvation and my glory: the rock of my strength, and my refuge, is in God." - Psalm 62:6-7

So do not fear, for I am with you; do not be dismayed, for I am your God. I will strengthen you and help you; I will uphold you with my righteous right hand. "All who rage against you will surely be ashamed and disgraced; those who oppose you will be as nothing and perish. Though you search for your enemies, you will not find them. Those who wage war against you will be as nothing at all.

Deliverance From The "CRAZY Blues"

I DECLARE AND DECREE, DELIVERANCE FROM ANXIETY AND FEAR IS YOUR NOW, TODAY, IN JESUS NAME! YOUR PAST TRAUMA WILL NOT KEEP YOU DOWN ANY LONGER! IN JESUS'S PRECIOUS NAME! GOD WILL KEEP HIS PROMISES! YOU WILL BE MADE WHOLE AGAIN! CRAZY BLUES WILL NO LONGER

KEEP YOU DOWN, YOUR CRAZY BLUES WILL CATUPULT YOU INTO PROSPERITY IN JESUS NAME! HALLELUJAH!

IT IS WRITTEN: GOD KNOWS THE PLANS HE HAS FOR YOU OF PROSPERITY! JEREMIAH 29:11

Yes, I was born into the Crazy Blues, raised in Dayton Ohio, and today thirty years now have passed and living in Dunedin Florida! I can say without a doubt my Father God truly is amazing. Yes, I am the daughter of the Most High God I AM, Minister of Prophetic dance inspired by Gospel and Blues, Arthur, Minister of Flag Dancing, Teacher of Prophetic Flag Dancing, and Owner of Healing In The Blues Non Profit Business, Owner of Wings Of Perez Publishing, and Author of "Waving The White Flag Respect The Gift".

God has delivered me from drama and the crazy blues! Hallelujah! I grew up in Dayton, Ohio a CRAZY town. It was there in this small country city town I was baptized in water at Tabernacle Baptist Church and later moved to Takoma Park, Maryland and Germantown Maryland.   I gave my life to Christ and I experienced a spiritual rebirth while attending Interdenominational Church of God in Gaithersburg Maryland. The Lord saved me from the crazy blues and a broken heart. I now go where the LORD sends me to speak about His glory and miracles in the blues.

It is written: The LORD is close to the brokenhearted and saves those who are crushed in spirit.

List what are your favorite songs of joy are.

1.

2.

3.

4.

5.

6.

7.

8.

NOW GIVE GOD GLORY!!

GOD is the Creator of the blues, and joy, so put off the old skins and put on the garments so you can get rid of certain kinds of blues.

God can use any one, all things, music, flags, harmonicas, guitars, scarfs, songs, dance, handkerchief, pictures, you and me to heal the land and his people for His glory. Glory Hallelujah!

It is written:

God knows the plans He has for you," declares the LORD, "plans to prosper you and not to harm you, plans to give you hope and a future.

Jeremiah 29:11

Move the Blues

The fresh air and warm sun are natural mood boosters. Your vitamins are all there! Exercise and count your blessings.

1. **Dive into the word.**
2. **Take every thought captive.**
3. **Put on praise music.**
4. **Put on spiritual songs.**
5. **Put on the blues song**

*God is an COMPOSER AND ARTIST
his creation is his masterpiece.*

*There are still promises over your life
speak to the mountain again!   Tell it
to move!*

God will work it out!

What are your goal for this year?

1.

2.

3.

YOU ARE GOD'S MASTERPIECE, A "JEWEL", YOU are Queens and Kings, cover yourself with BEAUTIFUL COLORS

Gold Light: A precious yellow metallic element, highly malleable and ductile, and not subject to oxidation or corrosion. Symbol: Au; atomic weight: 196.967; atomic number: 79; specific gravity: 19.3 at 20 degrees Celsius. A monetary standard. Symbolic of money, wealth, riches. Something likened to this metal in brightness, preciousness, superiority – as example: a heart of gold. A bright, metallic yellow color, sometimes tending toward brown. Spiritual metaphors: Divine Nature of YESHUA, Glory, Sacred to God, Faith of the Saints, Refining Process, Rare, Arrival, Passing the Test, Incorruptible, Pure, Authority, Kingship, Royalty, Richness, Excellence, Healing, and Compassion. A sample of Biblical scriptures:

HAVE FAITH AND BELIEVE

Because you have so little faith," He answered. "For truly I tell you, if you have faith the size of a mustard seed, you can say to this mountain, 'Move!

IT IS WRITTEN:

"MOVE, From here to there,' and it will move. Nothing will be impossible for you."
Matthew 17:20

The LORD is near to the brokenhearted; He saves the contrite in spirit. Many are the afflictions of the righteous, but the LORD delivers him from them all. He protects all his bones; not one of them will be broken....
Psalm 34:19

1.

God loves colors even the Blues!

Did you know that the color Blue signifies the celestial love of truth? That "blue" has this signification, is because it belongs to the color of the sky, and because by this color is signified truth from a celestial origin, which is truth from the good of love to the Lord.

This good reigns in the in most heaven, and in the middle or second heaven it is presented to view as crimson and blue; the good itself as crimson, and the derivative truth as blue. For in the other life, and in heaven itself, there appear most beautiful colors, all deriving their origin from good and truth. For the sphere of the affections of good and truth is sensibly presented before the eyes of angels and spirits by means of colors, and specific things by variously colored objects.

BE AWARE OF YOUR SURROUNDING

They are presented to the nostrils also by means of odors. For everything celestial, which is of good, and everything spiritual, which is of truth, is represented in the lower heavens by such things as appear in nature, thus to the very senses of the spirits and angels there. The reason why the spheres of the affection of good and truth are visibly presented by means of colors, is that the colors are modifications of heavenly light, thus of intelligence and wisdom.

Fine linen with embroidered work from Egypt was thy spread, that it might be to thee for a sign; blue and crimson from the isles of Elishah were thy covering.

These were thy traders with perfect things, with bales of blue and embroidered work, and with treasures of precious garments (Ezek. 27:7, 24);

Wear The Color of God's Glory

Beryl Light: A usually green or bluish green hexagonal mineral occurring as transparent to translucent prisms in igneous and metamorphic rocks. The most prevalent varieties are emeralds and aquamarines. Aquamarine may be found in Brazil, Madagascar, Kenya, Tanzania, Mozambique and Nigeria. Biblical history says, these gems are noted in Exodus 28:20 as the 10th Stone on the Priest's Ephod, in Ezekiel 1:16, 10:9, and 28:13 they are described in Ezekiel's Wheels, Daniel 10:6 lists this stone in Daniel's Vision and in Revelation 21:20 as the 8th foundation stone in the wall of New Jerusalem.

Brass Light: Bronze: Any of various alloys consisting essentially of copper and tin, the tin content not exceedingly 11 percent. A metallic brownish color. Brass: Any of various metal alloys consisting mainly of copper and zinc. A metallic yellow; lemon, amber, or reddish yellow color. Spiritual application: The Feet of YESHUA and HIS Perfect Judgment.

Amber Light: This color symbolizes the Fire of God and the Presence of God in addition to Harvest, Glory, Glory Cloud of Fire, The Brightness of HIS Presence, YESHUA as the Glory of God.   The fire of GOD is often recognized as an opportunity for YAHWEH to test the faith of HIS people and HIS faithfulness to walk with us through the fire storms of our lives.

Shine your Light

Every day we wear colors that resonate frequencies Even when we are not cognizant of their language. When we worship with flags or other worship instruments, the colors resonate frequencies. Even though we can see the some of the range of the colors, we cannot physically hear the sound of color frequencies.   All true worship frequencies send pleasure to heaven.

Be Aware of the light your carry!

Be Clearheaded, fervently pray, be hospitable towards one another, and remember as each one has received a gift bring it to the house of the Lord and minister the love of God to one another.

Cover yourself! COVER YOURSELF!

SPEAK LIFE OVER YOURSELF!

And finally, MEDITATE ON THESE DAILY AFFIRMATIONS

1. "The midst of your trail, struggles, and blues, God will show Himself in it!"
Pastor John P. Kee

2. "God will loose you from things and people, because they were not for you".

Pastor John P. Kee

3. "GOD IS A GOD THAT GOES BEFORE YOU.
Pastor John P. Kee

4. "God can not deny His word!"
Pastor John P. Kee

5. Some of the things you went through, was simply so God could loose you!
Pastor John P. Kee

…AND SURELY GOODNESS AND MERCY WILL FOLLOW YOU AND ME!